Circle Time Sessions for Relaxation and Imagination

Tony Pryce

P·C·P
Paul Chapman
Publishing

Paul Chapman Publishing
A SAGE Publications Company
1 Oliver's Yard
55 City Road
London
EC1Y 1SP

SAGE Publications Inc.
2455 Teller Road Thousand Oaks,
California 91320

SAGE Publications India Pvt Ltd.
B-42, Panchsheel Enclave
Post Box 4109
New Delhi 110 017

Commissioning Editors: George Robinson, Barbara Maines
Editorial Team: Mel Maines, Sarah Lynch.
Designer: Helen Weller
Cover Designer: Nick Shearn

A catalogue record for this book is available from the British Library

Library of Congress Control Number 2006901449

ISBN   13 978-1-4129-2018-6

Printed on paper from sustainable resources

Printed in Great Britain by The Cromwell Press Ltd, Trowbridge, Wiltshire

Contents

Foreword

The use of Circle Time has grown rapidly since the early 1990s, especially in primary schools. It should be seen as part of a whole-school provision to promote spiritual, moral, social and cultural development. As early as 1993, Robinson wrote:

> Schools should be aware that Circle Time can provide a forum for discussion of important issues: relationships, equal rights, friendship, freedom and justice, and is therefore an essential part of the National Curriculum. In the National Curriculum Council's discussion paper on Spiritual and Moral Development (1993) they state: 'It has to do with relationships with other people...it has to do with the universal search for individual identity, with our response to challenging experiences... It is to do with the search for meaning and purpose in life.' (page 2) Circle Time provides a vehicle by which children as individual members of a group can explore their experiences and individuality, balanced against the experiences and views of others. (Bliss et al 1993)

By 1995 Robinson was linking the elements of spiritual and moral development to the early writings of people such as Ballard (1982) who describes Circle Time as involving:

1. Awareness - knowing who I am.

2. Mastery - knowing what I can do (personal skills)

3. Social interaction - knowing how I function in the world of others (group and social skills).

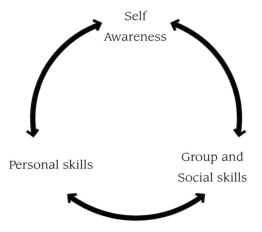

Self
Awareness

Personal skills

Group and
Social skills

Circle Time is an inter-related, interactive, multi-layered process. Within the circle participants learn about the self, learn about others and relate this knowledge to build relationships. (Bliss et al 1995)

If we take Ballard's assumptions from 1982 on what Circle Time does and relate this to what the National Curriculum's 1993 document on spiritual and moral development identifies as the essential requirements for young people:

Self-knowledge, relationships, feelings and emotions are an essential part of the spiritual and moral development of young people.

Self-knowledge: An awareness of oneself in terms of thoughts, feelings, emotions, responsibilities and experiences; a growing understanding and acceptance of individual identity; the development of self-respect.

Relationships: Recognising and valuing the worth of each individual; developing a sense of community; the ability to build up relationships with others.

Feelings and emotions: The sense of being moved by beauty or kindness; hurt by injustice or aggression; a growing awareness of when it is important to control emotions and feelings, and how to learn to use such feelings as a source of growth. (NCC1993)

We find remarkable similarities:

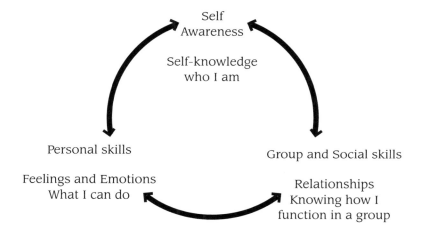

Self
Awareness

Self-knowledge
who I am

Personal skills

Group and Social skills

Feelings and Emotions
What I can do

Relationships
Knowing how I
function in a group

Taylor's research (2003) identified that Circle Time means different things to different people:

> *The Definition and implementation of Circle Time varies between schools, in terms of purpose, timing and the age of pupils involved, as well as how it is used and the type of resources. Some schools appear unaware of basic concepts such as sitting in a circle at the same level...* Taylor (2003)

She also noted in her research that though the majority of senior managers had claimed to have some training in Circle Time, it seemed that fewer class teachers in the case study schools had.

Training may only have been available to one or two staff in a given school, and fairly often this was very informal and consisted of 'watching others'.

She notes one teacher's comment:

> I have never seen it done on video or read about it. I have only
> just realised that I am doing 'Circle Time'... I probably just heard
> about it from classroom conversations, I can't remember. I've
> no resources on it and I've never done any training. I make up
> my own games. I didn't know that there were any resources.
> Really, I just do my own thing.

Similar comments are made to me when I run training days on
Circle Time. Some experienced users seem trapped into endless
rounds of talking about specific issues and desperately want to find
new elements to introduce to their circles. The ideas in this book
of introducing both relaxation and imagination techniques will
enrich Circle Time sessions and make it a more powerful tool to
assist emotional and social development.

George Robinson
Circle Time Author and Trainer

Introduction

I first became interested in teaching children visualisation techniques on a systematic basis when, after teaching what I had then termed a visualisation/meditation workshop (at an off-school residential site for children) a grandparent approached me and said, 'Thank you for teaching my grandchild meditation and visualisation. She has become a different person now. All she wants to do is go up to her room and do her meditation.' I received similar enthusiasm from children who persistently asked me when I was going to run another workshop. At that point I decided to run a series of lunchtime sessions which became very popular and well-attended.

I was further inspired when I had successes with children who exhibited challenging behaviour; children who, ordinarily, found it hard to sit still. I was particularly encouraged by one boy who normally had difficulty settling down to tasks. After one session he said to me, 'I quite enjoyed that.' I didn't need any more encouragement. I now teach these techniques quite readily whether I am in the classroom on a long-term basis or on a short visit.

What is visualisation?

In the context of this book, visualisation is the technique of using the imagination to create strong images, which are designed to enhance positive aspects of the self or personality. As Shakti (Gawain 2004), a person who has found great success in teaching her own version of visualisation to adults said, 'In Creative Visualisation, you use your imagination to create a clear image, idea or feeling of something you want to manifest.' (page 4)

This book has been created with the goal of helping children to manifest peace, calm, wellbeing and a healthy self-esteem.

We are all familiar with visualisation to one degree or another. We use a basic form of it when, for example, thinking about the meal we are going to make when we get home. The more we invest in the image the more it begins to impact on reality. The image then helps to influence our desire and vice versa. This results in us moving towards creating the meal we have visualised.

Another example of employment of a simple visualisation technique is by professional musicians. They will often mentally finger their instruments while sight-reading as a prelude to playing a tune for real.

Visualisation as a technique has appeared in many incarnations. One former Harley Street practitioner, Ronald Romark, developed a branch of it called Hypnothink. This is visualisation merged with hypnosis. He spent many years in a successful Harley Street practise healing people of all manner of phobias and other problems. He noted how visualisation could affect profound changes in an individual, stating that: 'Imagined success can equal real success. Intense imagination feeds a set of facts into the brain. Then when a future situation occurs, the personality reacts accordingly.' (Markham 1986 p33).

Let us not forget the use of visualisation as an aid in other medical areas ranging from fighting cancer to helping to combat stress and high blood pressure. Another area where visualisation is employed successfully is in the field of athletics. Athletes have enjoyed the benefits of visualisation techniques to help them become champions.

John Syer and Christopher Connolly use visualisation as a means of training top athletes such as cycling specialist Chris Boardman. He won a gold medal in the 1992 Olympic games in Atlanta,

USA. Syer and Connolly (1998) remarked that, visualisation of a physical action, process or state can affect your physical reality as can visualisation of an emotional state.' (page 46) They add later that, 'Visualisation is a skill. It is the process of watching yourself on a screen in your mind's eye, consciously evoking and guiding daydreams in which you appear towards a specific goal.

If visualisation is an activity that adults readily take up, why not start teaching children early so that the cultivation of their inner landscape becomes an integral part of their personal culture and habit of being? This will be another string to their bow that they can call upon to keep them steady during arduous times. Visualisation is a tool, which will allow them to appreciate, in time:

‣ how they can begin to work on their own self-esteem
‣ that there exist pockets of tranquillity within them that they can enhance at will with a little practice
‣ that their imagination is a powerful ally in their personal development.

The ideas in this book have been inspired by my experiences in several areas including:

‣ secondary/primary school teacher
‣ SEN worker
‣ working with nurture groups
‣ teacher of drama performance workshops
‣ play scheme worker
‣ a background in psychology and philosophy
‣ teaching visualisation exercises during lunchtimes and on school journeys.

The shape the book has taken has been informed by several observations.

When children who have a reputation for being disruptive are rewarded for being 'good' they often find praise hard to take. They will occasionally subvert this gain because it conflicts with their internal view of themselves or the external image that their fragile self-esteem has allowed them to build. It is as important to change the internal model as it to change the outer. Often those who find it hard to handle praise will go on a destructive path to re-establish the self they are comfortable with.

They seem to feel secure in their 'badness' and are often not sure who they will be without it. The self needs deep acceptance of possibilities and change, which need to be constantly reinforced.

Finding time within the demands of a crowded curriculum is difficult but it seems essential that we provide all young people with the skills of visualisation so we:

▸ Create the condition in which they can have a dialogue with their 'good' inner self. That self can be constituted around peace, a fruitful imagination, or simply be about a child feeling good about himself.

▸ Facilitate the development of a rich inner life of the child so that she can be more resourceful.

▸ Allow them to become accustomed to the idea of being inwardly successful.

▸ Help them to build an inner power of self-control and a confidence that they can work with and expand at will.

▸ Enable them to be a friend to themselves by facilitating the recognition that their inner world has rewarding things to offer. This will help them to become resourceful and not just rely on external factors to build up their self-esteem.

- ► Get them to practice and recognise that they have an inner world that it is as rich and important to develop as the outer one.

- ► Enable cultivation of positive inner self-image. Even with outer success people can still feel small if this is not complemented by a strong inner image or model. Body builders, for instance, despite a strong external physique, may suffer from reverse anorexia and still see themselves, internally, as that same stick-thin kid. The same is true of pop stars and any successful person who can often pull around an internal image of a bedraggled, insecure self that doesn't 'deserve' the success they have and will work to subvert this success, subconsciously at least.

- ► Help them to accommodate the idea that there is not just this one self they are heir to which is 'bad' but rather the self is like a mansion with many rooms and many resources within the rooms that perhaps need to be dusted down and made use of.

As so many schools now use Circle Time, it seems practical to introduce visualisation and relaxation techniques as an extra dimension to the sessions.

Circle Time and emotional health

There has been growing official emphasis on the benefits of emotional health and wellbeing of young people. The 'Every Child Matters' agenda and the National Healthy School initiative provide both an impetus and a framework for supporting emotional development. Evidence available at www.wiredforhealth.gov.uk/evidenceofimpact demonstrates that pupils who are healthy (in the widest sense):

- achieve more
- demonstrate a range of positive behaviours
- enhance their personal and social health.

The importance of developing healthy young people is not left to the discretion of the school:

> From September 2005 Ofsted will expect schools to demonstrate how they are contributing to the five national outcomes stipulated by Every Child Matters and the Children Act 2004:
>
> - being healthy
> - staying safe
> - enjoying and achieving
> - making a positive contribution
> - economic wellbeing.
>
> (National Healthy School Status)

Circle Time itself offers an ideal setting for carrying out these activities because of the recognition that a well-run circle offers a supportive and nurturing environment where children can readily explore issues, (emotional, personal and otherwise) that affect them.

The growing understanding amongst children about Circle Time as a 'special' and 'respected' space within the culture of the school can help to create the right ambience for carrying out these activities.

Introducing relaxation and visualisation (imagining) into Circle Time sessions

It's important to clarify how techniques such as relaxation, visualising and imagining fit into Circle Time. Lang (1998) identifies that a wide range of practices are all described as Circle Time. Taylor (2003) identifies:

> Some schools and some teachers use Circle Time spontaneously in response to problem behaviours. A few teachers expressed reservations about the possible negative effects of this approach:

> 'I think that my worry would be that if you use it too often it could be a bit blasé. 'Oh, we've got a problem, we're going to have a Circle Time!''

Ballard (1982) writes:

> Circle Time is not a therapy. It is not to be seen as a 'treatment' of any kind... we are not solving problems in a Circle Time session... The teacher does not bring to the circle a 'something is wrong and needs fixing' problem mentality.

The use of relaxation, visualization and imagining fits best with the following assumptions:

▸ Circle Time is a space within the school curriculum into which each person comes with unconditional acceptance.
▸ It is not the place for specific or individual problem-solving.
▸ It is not part of a school discipline system any more than the maths curriculum.

The structure of a typical session

It's preferable to have a circle of chairs, though if this is not convenient carpet squares provide a definite place for pupils to sit. This is especially important when doing activities that involve changing places.

Welcome

Welcome the children to the Circle and remind them of the rules. Children can be involved in setting the rules. These often include the following:

‣ We listen when someone else is speaking.
‣ We may pass.
‣ We don't remind anyone else what they should be doing.
‣ There are no put-downs.

(Bliss et al 1995)

Warm-ups

These are usually activities that involve some movement that helps mix the group up, so pupils will be sitting next to the people that they don't usually sit with.

Introduction to the theme

Each theme has a series of discussion points to start the session off. These could be used as either sentence completion, going round the circle with each individual making a statement, or in pairs with each dyad discussing the question/statement for a couple of minutes before going round the circle with one of the pair briefly describing their discussion.

Some of the themes have an activity sheet which could be done before the session and used to prompt discussion.

The Theme

The relaxation, visualisation and imagining activity will form the main focus of the session. After the activity, discussion can take place in pairs or using sentence completion on both the specific theme and the technique of relaxing, imagining etc.

Closing activity

A game such as 'Pass a Smile', a gentle hand-squeeze passed around the circle or a group round of applause all give a positive end to the session.

The visualisation exercises can also complement activities such as Physical Education as a means of getting children to settle down. They can be used in the morning as a focus for getting the day started on a positive note or at any time when a period of calm is required. As a teacher myself, I know there is not always the time to fit things in during the busy day. When time is short it is possible to carry out the exercises by leaving out the deeper relaxation technique. It is more beneficial to carry out the exercises than to forego them just because you can't fit them in their entirety.

This book can be used with children from primary school age upwards. I have carried out the exercises with five year old children through to adults. The only requirement for participation is that they are at an age where they are able to understand the nature of the exercises.

Preparations for relaxing, imagining and visualisations

Encourage the children to be as relaxed as possible with an upright posture. There is not necessarily any need to adopt special postures. I have carried out these exercises with the children sat cross-legged on the floor as well as sat upright in a chair.

At the end of the exercises I always end by asking the children to send some symbolic light or gift into the world as a goodwill gesture, one that encourages them to think of others. This in turn helps them to recognise themselves as important contributors to the world.

Ask the children how they feel about the exercises after they have carried them out. If they find certain visualisations difficult, such as seeing themselves celebrating success, then this can be important feedback, offering areas for sensitive exploration. For example, a child having difficulty with visualising success might indicate that their self-esteem is such that they have difficulty either seeing the good in their life or celebrating their successes. You might even encourage the child to keep a diary reflecting on any changes.

Countdown

Try to count out of the visualisation, especially where activities are time-limited. This allows the child time to adjust to the rhythm of the world as well as conquer a reluctance to come out of an enjoyable experience.

Pauses during the exercise

I have placed pauses at strategic points of the exercises. These are meant to allow time for the children to build up and appreciate the images they are creating as well as to derive feelings such as that of peace from them. You can use your own judgement as to when you think it appropriate to add more pauses. The exercises can also be expanded or contracted as time permits.

Questions for exploration

The following are questions you can ask for ongoing exploration and feedback:

- Were you able to create strong visual images?
- Were you able to create positive feelings?
- How did the exercise make you feel?
- Did you find the exercise easy to get into?
- Did you learn anything about yourself from doing the exercise?
- Have any of the exercises that we have done previously helped at all in everyday life? For instance, have any of them helped you to become calmer, more focused, confident, or understanding?

Diary

If you are able to carry out these activities as an ongoing project you could encourage the children to keep a visualisation diary so that they can monitor their progress and how their feelings moods, behaviour and confidence are changing.

The activity sheets can be used as a way of both guiding a child towards a positive outlook as well as acting as a prompt for monitoring his wellbeing.

I also believe that it is important for children have a vision of the type of person they would like to be so that this isn't all left to the sculpting that life will carry out.

This work helps children to develop strong imaginations because so much of it is built on creating internal images. This is quite a healthy antidote for the child; brought up in the Play Station age in which the imaginative is frequently housed in a plastic box rather than in their own minds.

All of the exercises (apart from Ball of Light which is intended for group use) are suitable for use with one child as well as a group of children.

Activity sheets

I have made suggestions for the use of these resource sheets around particular exercises. However, they can also be used either independently of these activities, with other activities or as an exercise in and of themselves. To photocopy the worksheets directly from this book, set your photocopier to enlarge by 125% and align the edge of the page to be copied against the leading edge of the copier glass (usually indicated by an arrow).

Discussion and bullet point prompts

These are meant as guides only and can be incorporated, adapted and used in conjunction with your own questions. You may decide that some are surplus to requirements in relation to your knowledge of the child or children, their understanding or even in relation to the time you have at your disposal. The discussion prompts can be used as Circle Time material in their own right

Developing your own exercises

The ten sessions in the book should provide a framework for you to develop skills and confidence in using these techniques. Once you feel confident you are only limited by your imagination as to how you can use your new skills. Don't feel that these can only be used in Circle Time – they will be appropriate in other contexts, from relaxing before stressful situations to stimulus for creative writing.

A Relaxation Exercise

The following is a question you might ask in order to promote discussion:

▸ How do you relax?
▸ What are the benefits, if any, to relaxation?

The exercise that follows is one that I use to help children to relax before the visualisation begins. You might like to include some relaxation techniques of your own.

This relaxation technique, as with the visualisation or visualisation exercises, can be carried out either sitting in a chair or sitting on the floor.

You can begin and complete the relaxation exercise by reciting the following words to the children:

I want you make sure that you are sitting comfortably to begin with. Sit upright and erect without straining the body. I want you to imagine that there is a string attached to your head. The string is being pulled gently and your head is now being pulled up and your back is beginning to straighten. Hold this position in as relaxed a manner as possible because we don't want any tension in the body. Now I want you to direct your attention to the very end of your toes. From here we are going to talk the body into relaxing and letting go of any tension, which we often build up even without realising it.

Become aware of your toes and make sure there is no tension. Say to your toes, 'Toes relax.' I want you to now think of your attention as a searchlight whose job is to sweep across the whole body highlighting any tension whilst increasing the relaxation. Think of tension as a criminal element that is trying to escape detection. Your job as a detective is to take it out of circulation: to arrest it. Slowly allow your searchlight attention to move up the body stopping at key points of the body where tension normally hides. Make sure the area around the ankle is now relaxed.

(Pause)

Your searchlight is now moving. It is now focused on the calf muscles, the area behind the back of the ankle and the back of the knees. Tell that area to relax.

(Pause)

Now I want you to slowly move your searchlight attention up through the body, making sure each area you attend to is relaxed. Stop at the area above your knees, the thighs, and make sure the whole of the front and back of the thighs are relaxed. You can do a little check by contracting, squeezing or tightening the muscles in the thighs and then slowly letting go of the squeeze. The diminishing of the squeeze should be the point at which the muscle is most relaxed.

Take a moment to enjoy this aspect of understanding your body.

(Pause)

Move your attention to the top of the thighs. Ask this area and the area behind the thighs (your bottom) to relax. Now move your attention until you get to the area around the stomach. This is an important area to be aware of because we register a lot of discomfort and intense emotional feeling there such as butterflies and anxiety. Make sure that there is no muscular tension in either the front or the back of the body. Ask this area to relax.

(Pause)

Now move your attention searchlight slowly up the body until you get to the chest - another important area because this is where the lungs and the heart are housed. Check that your breathing is smooth and regular. This area is also a good tool of communications which offers us feedback for how we are feeling. When we are angry, fearful or anxious our breathing becomes shorter and we often end up breathing in the higher part of the chest. Breathing more deeply can help us to remain more at ease emotionally.

Check that your heartbeat is not too fast which can be an indicator of stress and tension and anxiety. Check for any signs of tension. Direct your searchlight towards the neck. Tension is registered particularly the area at the back. This is where we get the expression 'pain in the neck'. Ask this area to relax. Now I want you to direct your attention towards the head. Relax this area. Check your mouth is relaxed, that the eyebrows aren't pushed together or the forehead isn't scrunched up due to concentrating too hard. Ask this area to relax. Sit and enjoy the feelings. This will help you to get to know your body well so that gradually you'll come to sense when it is relaxed and when it isn't.

(Pause)

You may feel a slight tingling sensation as you feel the blood flowing through your body. It is a revelation; something you have now discovered about your body that you might not have came across before. The body is also showing you how you are most alive – something we might not necessarily think about when we are going about our business.

Just recognising the fact that we are alive (and not taking this fact for granted) and that the body has its own way of telling us this, can be a fantastic and wondrous discovery.

I will count from one to ten. At the end of the count you can slowly open your eyes. Once your eyes are open I want you to just gently adjust to what is around you. Don't jump up suddenly or start talking. I also want you appreciate any differences in how your body is feeling from the way it felt before. (Begin the count).

At the end of the exercise discuss with the class:

▸ How did this make you feel?
▸ Was it easy?
▸ What part was difficult?
▸ Could you use this relaxation method by yourself?

Row Your Boat

This session uses a visualisation for building inner peace and generating good feeling.

The following questions can be used to promote discussion:

▸ What does inner peace mean to you?

▸ How can inner peace help you and others in everyday life?

Visualisation exercise

Initiate the relaxation exercise or your own suitable method.

Now you can begin and complete the visualisation exercise by reciting the following words to the children:

I want you to imagine that you are in the boat on the sea. You are lying in the boat gazing up at the sky. The boat is moving gently through the water. As the boat goes through the water you realise it has a rhythm; a gentle rocking rhythm as it is moved by the waves lapping against it sides. Each time the boat rocks gently I want you to imagine that it is soothing you. It is taking away any mental tension you might have. I want you to feel the mental tension going away. The boat continues to rock gently. I want you to imagine that it is rocking away any worries you have and anything that stops you being able to achieve your very best. I am going to give you some time to enjoy the gentle rocking of the boat

(Pause)

The slow motion of the boat makes you feel relaxed and at ease with yourself. I want you to take in all this goodness. Soak it up as though you are a sponge.

(Pause)

You look up at the sun amidst the blue sky. I want you to imagine that the sun notices that you are there. It likes you and in order to show its appreciation of you it sends a beam of coloured light towards you. The light touches you and you feel its warmth throughout your whole body. It makes you feel very good.

(Pause)

I want you to keep hold of this feeling. It is the sun's gift to you.

You begin to notice that the boat is slowing down. It gently comes to a stop. You stand up and you realise that you are now on a small island. You decide to get out of the boat and go for a walk.

You look down and see that beneath you, gently cushioning your feet, is a type of sand that you have never ever seen before. It is made up of beautiful colours. You also notice that as you walk along, the sand tickles your feet and leaves you with a magical feeling. It makes you feel happy. You walk along and you see shells on the floor. They are coloured the brightest purple. They even seem to radiate friendliness. You move towards one and pick it up. As soon as you do this you feel a warm glow throughout your entire body. This glow makes you feel very, very special and well-liked.

(Pause)

It is life's gift to you when all is as it should be.

It is time to go now. You walk back slowly to the boat. There is a tiny shell in the boat, a gift for you to take back and share with others. You sit back in the boat.

I want you to think of some person or some part of the world that you would like to share this warmth with. Send them a little of what you have. Imagine a way that you could send them this feeling of warmth. For instance you could imagine projecting or sending that feeling into an object that you offer as a gift. It is your own special gift. If you can't imagine a way to send this good feeling then send it as a ray of light. I also want you to take some of the feeling with you to keep as your own.

I will count from one to ten. At the end of the count you can slowly open your eyes. Once your eyes are open I want you to just gently adjust to what is around you. Don't jump up suddenly or start talking. I also want you appreciate any differences in how your body is feeling from the way it felt before. (Begin the count).

At the end of the exercise discuss with the class:

▶   How did this make you feel?
▶   Was it easy?
▶   What part was difficult?
▶   Could you use this relaxation method by yourself?

Use the visual activity sheet Inner Peace to represent the feelings that were experienced by class members.

Inner Peace

Use this space to show your inner peace,
in any way you wish.

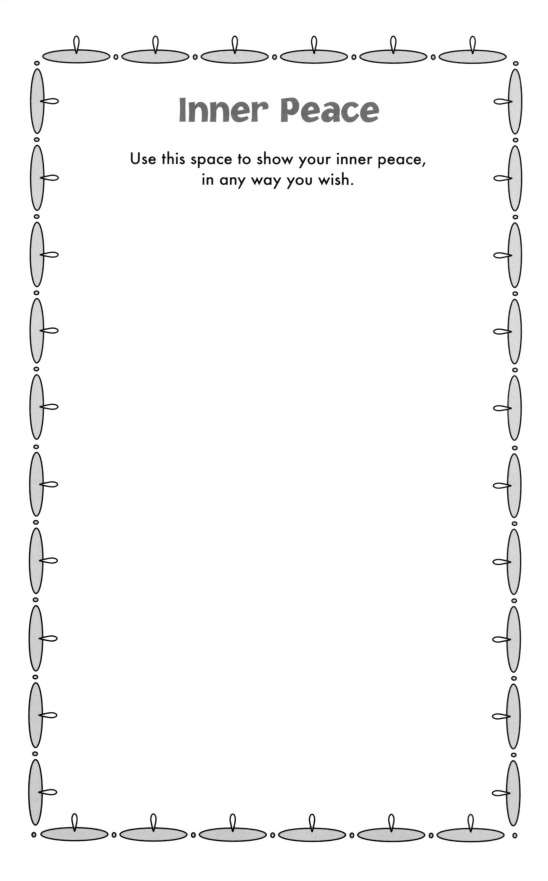

The Giant Within

This is a visualisation for making the inner self bigger. The following paragraph is intended for the purposes of generating discussion.

Sometimes people who aren't confident or who don't feel good about themselves on the inside refer to themselves as feeling 'small'. If on the inside you were to rate yourself, in terms of size, how would you see yourself? Do you see yourself as big as a giant, tiny as a mouse or just a normal size?

You can explore the issue further with these additional questions:

▸ What happens when we feel small inside?
▸ How do we carry ourselves?
▸ Does feeling small inside have any influence on our actions or behaviour?
▸ What happens when we feel large inside?

Additional note

You might like to discuss with the children that people often have an internal model or picture of who they think they are. Despite the fact that someone may act tough on the outside this can be at odds with their internal world. Inside they might feel very small. It is often said that bullies are actually small people who want to make up for a lack of confidence. It is also said that many bullies were victims of bullying themselves. Both of these statements are sometimes true.

Discuss with them that some pop stars, for instance, despite their external image of power and wealth, can feel quite vulnerable.

Explore with the children how they really feel about themselves as well as how they would like to feel about themselves. Relate to the children that this inner character or model, whether we are aware of it or not, often acts as a driver for our actions in life just like the driver of the car will make the car go where he or she wants it to go. Similarly, our inner model can make us do things based upon how we feel.

Pre-visualisation exercise

As a warm-up ask the children to remember any good feelings they have experienced generally. Explain to the children that they are going to use the memory of good feelings in order to project images into their mediation just like a person might charge a battery with energy.

Visualisation exercise

Initiate the relaxation exercise or your own suitable method.

Now you can begin and complete the visualisation exercise by reciting the following words to the children:

As you begin to feel more relaxed I want you to have an image of yourself from the inside. I want you to really see yourself. I want you to project all the warm feelings you can towards this image of yourself. Imagine this image of you is smiling. The more you project warm feelings towards this image the more this image is smiling.

(Pause)

Something else begins to happen. You notice that this image of you is beginning to grow. You encourage this growth by sending towards it more love and warmth. This inner image begins to grow

26

and grow. It keeps growing until it is as big as a house then it grows further until it is as big as a tree.

(Pause)

This is now you. This giant is you when you feel warmth towards yourself, when you accept yourself for who you are, when you are kind towards yourself and feel at ease with yourself and at peace. Try and appreciate how powerful this can make you feel. You feel bigger than the bad feelings you sometimes have. You feel bigger than comments people might make about you. You feel bigger than those feelings that come with not quite living up to other people's expectations. You feel bigger than the problems in the world. When you feel like a giant you can recover more easily from the disappointments and setbacks that are part of life.

(Pause)

Imagine now moving about the world, strutting around as this giant. You are looking at the world from a great height and you no longer feel swallowed up by it. This makes you feel great inside. With each step you take you feel more secure and more sure of yourself. Other people can't make you feel small. Hold onto this feeling of being a giant. Allow this feeling to travel throughout your entire body.

(Pause).

As you walk about as this giant you see a boy. He is trying to reach up and to pick an apple. Because you feel so powerful you feel you have enough good feeling to want to help him so you give him a lift up the tree. You are now beginning to realise that you can accomplish anything that you really set your mind to. Take one of these apples yourself. Imagine giving it to someone or offering it as a gift to a part of the world that you think will need it.

I will count from one to ten. At the end of the count you can slowly open your eyes. Once your eyes are open I want you to just gently adjust to what is around you. Don't jump up suddenly or start talking. I also want you appreciate any differences in how your body is feeling from the way it felt before. (Begin the count.)

At the end of the exercise discuss with the class:

- How did this make you feel?
- Was it easy?
- What part was difficult?
- Could you use this relaxation method by yourself?

Use the visual activity sheet Feeling Good Inside to represent what feelings were experienced by class members.

Feeling Good Inside

Use this space in any way you like to show
feeling good inside yourself.

The House That Peace Built

This is a visualisation on finding a peaceful space within.

The following paragraph is intended to prompt discussion.

We are a collection of qualities which include our personality, habits, character, and way of being, thinking and acting. We are like a mansion with many rooms. There are many interesting things in the rooms. When we are aware of all the things in the room we can make use of them more easily. It is far too easy to focus on that one less than perfect aspect of ourselves. On the other hand, other parts of ourself can become neglected like forgotten things in rooms which gather dust. For instance, one part of a person may be quite aggressive when dealing with people but might be kind to animals. The side that cares for animals can be built up to include caring for people.

The following questions can be used to explore the topic further:

▸ Who do you think you are (in terms of your qualities)?
▸ Are there many parts to ourselves?
▸ Are we ever all bad or all good?
▸ Are we a collection of lots of qualities?
▸ What do you think one of your good qualities is?

Visualisation exercise

Initiate the relaxation exercise or your own suitable method.

Now you can begin and complete the visualisation exercise by reciting the following words to the children:

You are going for a walk. Each step you take on the ground is like treading on feathers. Every step makes you feel very comfortable. Each step makes you feel happier and happier.

(Pause)

As you are walking along a house starts to come into view. There is something special about the house. It seems to give off a light, which attracts you to it. It somehow feels warm and inviting. It has a garden with the most beautiful flowers that you can imagine of every description and colour. You stop to take in the wonderful sight.

(Pause)

You enter into the garden and as you get close to the flowers they send out beams of sparkling colour of every description that rest gently upon your skin. Each time the beams of colour touch you it makes you feel wanted, special and loved.

(Pause)

The house looks inviting. You reach for the door handle, which sparkles as you touch it. The door opens into a hallway. You begin to walk up the stairs. Every step that you take makes you feel calmer, more peaceful and more relaxed.

(Pause)

There is a room from which a bright light is emanating. As soon as you enter the room you feel a deep sense of peace. There is a chair in the corner. You go to sit down to take in the radiance of the room. The chair is so soft you feel as though you are sitting on air. You breathe deeply and each time you do you breathe in the radiance and warmth of the room feel more relaxed and peaceful.

(Pause).

 It is time to return. As you begin to leave the house you realise that there is something in your pocket. You look down only to discover that it is a ball made up of light. It is sparkling so brightly that it is warming up your face with its radiance. It is a gift to remind you of the house and that the room in the house is your very own special place of peace. It is your special place inside of yourself that you can return to in order to obtain peace and a sense of wellbeing. I want you to imagine some of the light rubbing off the ball. It is like stardust. Send it to some place or someone in the world who you think could benefit from it.

I will count from one to ten. At the end of the count you can slowly open your eyes. Once your eyes are open I want you to just gently adjust to what is around you. Don't jump up suddenly or start talking. I also want you appreciate any differences in how your body is feeling from the way it felt before. (Begin the count.)

At the end of the exercise discuss with the class:

▸ How did this make you feel?
▸ Was it easy?
▸ What part was difficult?
▸ Could you use this relaxation method by yourself?

Either use 'My Identity' activity sheet or 'Feeling Calm' sheet to represent what feelings were experienced by class members.

My Identity

Our self, with all the qualities that we possess, is like a house with many articles in it. The articles in the house make up the house's identity. All the qualities that we possess help to make up our identity. In the spaces below, write down as many of the positive qualities that you can think of that you possess. For example: 'I have a good sense of humour,' or 'I am caring'. Be generous.

Feeling Calm

Use the space below in any way you want to show
feeling calm inside yourself.

Mirror Mirror On My Wall

During this session you will be using a visualisation exercise that focuses on accepting and loving ourselves for who we are.

The following questions can be used to promote discussion:

▸ What does it mean to love yourself?
▸ Why is this important?
▸ Can we accept ourselves for who we are?
▸ How do people who like themselves behave in the world?
▸ What is self-esteem?
▸ Do you know of any examples of people who have a high self-esteem?

Visualisation exercise

Initiate the relaxation exercise or your own suitable method.

Now you can begin and complete the visualisation exercise by reciting the following words to the children:

I want you to imagine that you are in a room. It is a room with nicely coloured walls. The atmosphere is very pleasant in the room and you feel welcomed. You begin to feel really relaxed in this space. Rays of sunlight pour through the open window to greet you. As you walk towards the window the rays of multi-coloured sunlight catch you.

(Pause)

The light contains so much goodness, the same type of goodness that you might feel when you've been out on a trip or something has excited you. As the light brushes your skin the goodness from the light starts to travel all over your body enveloping it like a soft blanket. This makes you feel more and more relaxed and very good about yourself.

(Pause)

As you walk around the room you notice that the room isn't empty. There is a mirror on the wall. You approach the mirror and you can see that just like all mirrors it seems to show you your reflection. Have a good look at your image. As you look more closely you notice that your image is smiling at you much more than you were doing. This is no ordinary mirror, this is a magic mirror. The smile is big and cheerful and warm. It almost makes you want to laugh with joy. This is a very happy face.

(Pause)

As you look into the mirror you notice that you cannot help but smile too. The more you gaze at the image the more you begin to look like this image. Your smile begins to grow until you look exactly like that cheerful, joyful face that is staring at you. This image gives you a very good feeling. You feel great warmth, starting in the facial area then travelling throughout your entire body, making your body feel as light as air. (Pause to allow the children to absorb the experience.)

It is now time to leave the mirror behind for another day. Before you do I want you to think of someone or a part of the world that you would like to share your good feelings or this warmth with. Send them a little of what you have. See if you can find an imaginative way of doing this. For instance, you could imagine projecting or sending that feeling into an object that you offer as a gift. It is your own special gift. If you can't imagine a way to send this good feeling then send it as a ray of light. I also want you to take something with you of the feeling to keep as your own.

I will count from one to ten. At the end of the count you can slowly open your eyes. Once your eyes are open I want you to gently adjust to what is going on around you. Try to look at the world with freshness and discovery as though you are seeing it for the first time. I also want you appreciate any differences in how your body is now feeling from the way it felt before. (The count down begins.)

At the end of the exercise discuss with the class:

▸   How did this make you feel?
▸   Was it easy?
▸   Which part was difficult?
▸   Could you use this relaxation method by yourself?

Either use 'My Ideal Reflection' activity sheet or 'Feeling Happy' activity sheet to represent which feelings were experienced by class members.

My Ideal Reflection

What would you like to be like on the inside? How would you like to feel inside or think? Write your vision of yourself on the lines of the mirror.

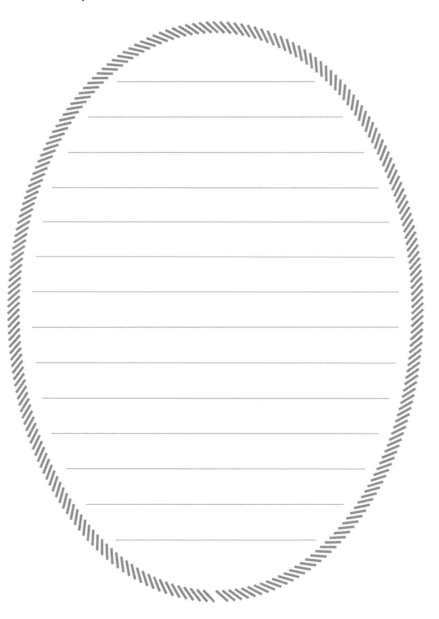

Feeling Happy

Use the space below in any way you want to show
yourself feeling happy inside.

The Happy Forest

This is an exercise based on generating warmth and goodwill towards ourselves.

The following is a short story, which is intended for discussion.

David Adams felt that he couldn't do anything right. To his mind he was no good at anything. He liked nothing about himself and found it almost impossible to praise himself for anything that he did. He gave himself no positive attention whatsoever and found it hard to get it from those around him because he reacted negatively to others. He didn't think that he had any nice qualities at all. Gradually, he started to gain the attention of a group of older, more experienced boys. These boys began to influence him. David thought they liked him. However the boys had other things on their mind. Gradually they used David to create mischief which included stealing money from people.

Further discussion can be generated with the uses of these questions:

‣   How do you think David is feeling about himself?
‣   Why is David acting in this way?
‣   What can be done to help him?

Visualisation exercise

Initiate the relaxation technique or your own suitable method.

Now you can begin and complete the visualisation exercise by reciting the following words to the children:

I want you to imagine that you are walking in a green field. The green colour of the grass seems to sparkle like an emerald with each step that you take. You are walking at a slow, gentle and relaxed pace. It is as thought you are walking on a cushion of air. With every step you take you feel more and more peaceful. With every step you take any worry, ill feeling or hurt is draining away through your body to your feet and is being absorbed by the earth.

(Pause)

As you are walking along, feeling more and more relaxed, a forest comes into your vision. It seems to shimmer with a brightness that you have not seen before. It attracts you so you walk towards it. You are met by trees that seem to be 100 feet tall. Although they don't make a sound, in their silence they seem to be greeting you. The trees are directing all their warmth towards you. They are very friendly. Every tree you can see seems to glisten with radiant colour. You can't wait to touch a tree. As you do you feel the warmth of the tree begin to travel throughout your whole body, making you feel very good about yourself.

(Pause)

You begin to walk on. You hear a bird singing the sweetest of songs imaginable. This adds further to your pleasant feeling.

(Pause)

You look around for the bird and there you see it. Its feathers are made up the richest purple, orange and red. Just looking at it makes you feel a sense of wonder. To your amazement it flies from the tree and perches on your shoulder. It makes you feel very secure and safe. The bird begins to chatter. As you listen more carefully you realise that you can understand its language. It seems to be telling you to think good things about yourself and like yourself for who you are. You stay with the bird for a while because it brings you peace.

(Pause)

It is now time to leave the forest and come back to your surroundings. The bird accompanies you to the end of the forest. It flies to the ground, picks up a seed and places it in your open hand. It is a gift to remind you to think pleasant things about yourself and to love and appreciate yourself for who you are. You break a piece off and send it to a place or individual that needs it.

I will count from one to ten. At the end of the count you can slowly open your eyes. Once your eyes are open I want you to gently adjust to what is around you. Don't jump up suddenly or start talking. I also want you appreciate any differences in how your body is feeling from the way it felt before. (Begin the count).

At the end of the exercise discuss with the class:

- ▸ How did this make you feel?
- ▸ Was it easy?
- ▸ Which part was difficult?
- ▸ Could you use this relaxation method by yourself?

Use the 'Feeling Safe' activity sheet to represent feelings that were experienced by class members.

Feeling Safe

Use the space below in any way you want to show yourself feeling safe inside.

Sky Dance With An Eagle

~~~~~~~~~~~~~~~~~~~~

This is an exercise for developing inner peace and wellbeing. The following questions can be used to promote discussion:

‣ What does 'peaceful' mean?
‣ Do you have a special place where you feel peaceful?
‣ What stops you from feeling peaceful?

Visualisation exercise

Initiate the relaxation exercise or your own suitable method.

Now you can begin and complete the visualisation exercise by reciting the following words to the children:

I want you to use your strongest powers of imagination to imagine that you are sat by a stream. The water in the stream flows by quietly. The very slow hushing, slushing, rushing sound that the river is making is like the sound of music.

(Pause)

You listen to the sound and come to realise that with each flowing movement of the stream you are becoming more relaxed. Any problems you have are flowing away with the river. It seems to be able to absorb all your difficulties, all your anxieties and all your concerns only to wash them away. It is a very special river with healing powers. It makes you feel at peace with yourself as well as at peace with those around you.

(Pause)

There are snow-topped mountains to the side of you. They look beautiful to the eye and you begin to wonder about what mysteries and secrets they hold. When you look at the mountains they make you feel very happy.

(Pause)

You look up and on top of the mountain you see a huge eagle; the king of the sky. It notices you and although you don't know how, it seems to smile at you. It spreads its great majestical wings and as it does the colour of its feathers glisten like the colour in a rainbow. It begins to take off. It soars high above the air and circles overhead. Every time it circles, as if by magic, you begin to feel more at peace.

(Pause)

The bird is inviting you to fly. It is saying to you that all you need is a little imagination. You spread your arms and before you know it you are at the side of the eagle. Now you know why eagles spend so much time in the sky – it is because the sky is a very peaceful place to be. The bird guides you over the most fantastic and wondrous scenery; over lakes that shine, valleys with luscious fruit trees and fields of sparkling green grass.

(Pause)

It is time to go now and the bird guides you back down to earth. You land gently. You thank the eagle and it goes on its way. As you turn to leave, you notice a feather on your shoulder. In the light you see that it is made up of the most fantastic colours that you have ever seen. You blow on it and some of the colourful bits of feather float in the air. Send these to someone or a place in the world that needs it.

I will count from one to ten. At the end of the count you can slowly open your eyes. Once your eyes are open I want you to just gently adjust to what is around you. Don't jump up suddenly or start talking. I also want you appreciate any differences in how your body is feeling from the way it felt before. (Begin the count.)

At the end of the exercise discuss with the class:

- How did this make you feel?
- Was it easy?
- Which part was difficult?
- Could you use this relaxation method by yourself?

Use the 'Imagination' activity sheet to represent the feelings that were experienced by class members.

Imagination

Use the space below in any way you want to show
your imagination.

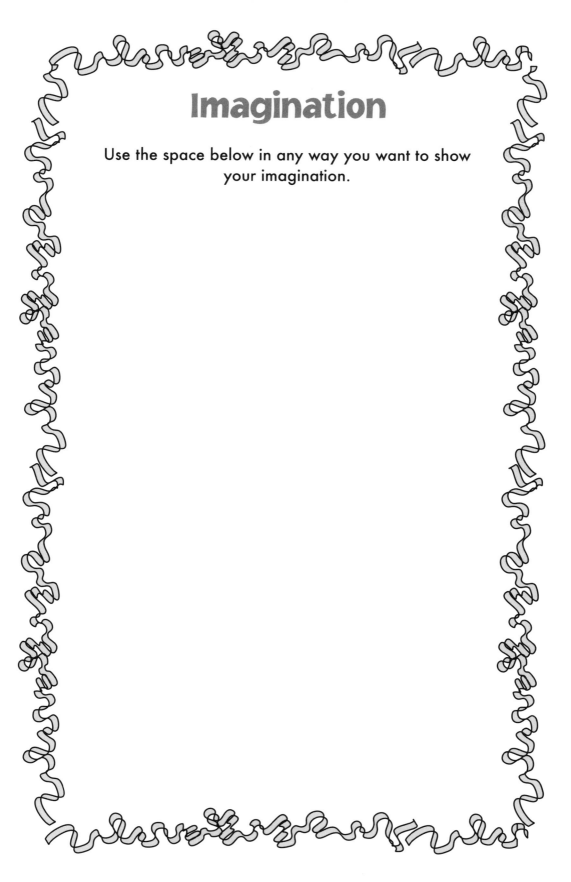

Butterfly Valley

This is a visualisation based on building confidence.

The following questions can be used in order to explore this topic:

- What does confidence mean to you?
- Can you think of other words for confidence?
- How would you describe a person who is confident?
- How would you describe the body language of a confident person?

One of the issues that can be touched upon is that confident people have a sense of self-assurance. They walk with their head held high as though not afraid to face the world or the challenges that face them. They can appear fearless.

Visualisation exercise

Initiate the relaxation exercise or your own suitable method.

Now you can begin and complete the visualisation exercise by reciting the following words to the children:

I want you to imagine that you are taking a slow walk in a place where there are hills at either side of you. These hills are nature's big brother and sister. Their presence feels like a great big comforting hug or embrace; the kind we all need from time to time. In this place you are surrounded by tall, elegant trees and bushes of vibrant green that seems to shimmer with the joys of life. There are small flowers of so many varieties of colours that they remind you of a rainbow. It is plain to see that this is a very good place to be.

(Pause)

As you walk you come across a pebbled path lined with small trees. You follow the path which leads downward. As you walk on further you can hear the sound of running water. Its gentle trickling makes you feel very peaceful and calm. This calm begins to go through your whole body, from your head to your toes.

(Pause)

You follow the path down. It leads you to a waterfall. The water is crystal clear and sparkles with the warm brilliance of diamonds. There are trees at the side of the water.

Something gently catches your attention. You look towards the tree and it looks as though the bark of the tree is moving. You look closely and see that the movement is caused by small butterflies, thousands of them, on the tree. One of the butterflies sees you and begins to fly. Once it takes to the air and fully expands its wing you can see that the inner parts of its wings are coloured the brightest orange. This is a rare treat because these butterflies normally like to remain camouflaged and will only reveal their true colours to people they trust.

You begin to realise that the more relaxed and peaceful you become the more the butterfly comes towards you. Others start to leave the tree and come towards you as they recognise your peace and calmness. Very soon there are hundreds of bright butterflies gently circling around you. Some begin to land on you and as they do you start to make you feel really good about yourself and happy within yourself.

You are feeling really confident and alive with joy. You feel that you could handle any situation without crumbling.

(Pause)

The more joyful and happy you feel the more they begin to dance about you. They are dancing to the rhythm of your own happy song that comes from your heart.

(Pause)

It is time to go now. One by one the butterflies return to their home on the tree. However, there is one which accompanies you on your way out. With all the grace of a feather in a breeze, the butterfly flutters over to a pool of water on the ground. You decide to put your hand in the water. When you take your hand out of the pool all the water trickles off it apart from one tiny drop. To your amazement this drop turns itself into a tiny diamond from which light of every colour cascades like a rainbow-coloured waterfall. This diamond is a gift to you; a symbol of your peace, happiness and growing confidence. Share some of it with the world by directing a ray of this light to a place or person that needs it.

I will count from one to ten. At the end of the count you can slowly open your eyes. Once your eyes are open I want you to gently adjust to what is around you. Don't jump up suddenly or start talking. I also want you appreciate any differences in how your body is feeling from the way it felt before. (Begin the count.)

At the end of the exercise discuss with the class:

▸ How did this make you feel?
▸ Was it easy?
▸ Which part was difficult?
▸ Could you use this relaxation method by yourself?

Either use the 'My Butterfly' activity sheet or 'Feeling Confident' activity sheet to represent the feelings that were experienced by class members.

My Butterfly

When we have confidence we feel that we can achieve many things. Write on the butterfly the areas in which you would like to be more confident. For example, making new friends, standing up for yourself, speaking out in class or making yourself heard.

Feeling Confident

Use the space below in any way you want to show
yourself feeling confident inside.

Thought Balloons

This session includes an exercise for learning to let go of troublesome thought.

The following is an analogy comparing thought to balloons in a fairground. It can be used to support the visualisation.

A fairground analogy

This particular visualisation is called 'Thought Balloons' and is going to be based on thought itself. Have you ever been to a carnival or fair and seen people selling all kinds of balloons filled with gas that makes them float? The balloons come in all sorts of shapes and sizes. There are some shaped as animals and there are others with faces on them. The balloons are thin, fat, oval and round. They also come in a variety of colours.

Imagine what would happen if the balloon seller was to let them all go. There would be balloons of every description flying around the carnival or fairground. If you decided to go after them you might get lucky. You might be able to catch hold of a fat one or an orange one or the one shaped as a dog. However, some might be too full of gas to catch and would go whizzing off into the clouds. You might find a big group of them together and to take hold of them whilst they lift you off the ground and take you to a place you don't want to be.

Additionally, whilst you are being distracted by the balloons you might be missing something else that is far more interesting going on in the background such as the appearance of the red fire engine.

The reason I am telling you this story, in preparation for our thought visualisation, is to demonstrate how much our thoughts can act rather like the balloons in the story.

Our thoughts come in every shape size and colour. Some thoughts stay around for a short time whilst others float around in our minds throughout the day. And just like the balloons at a fairground there are some we really like and some we don't like.

During the course of the day all kinds of thought balloons appear in our head caused by various kinds of influences both inside and outside of ourselves. Like the balloons in a fairground sometimes the mind just chases them and tries to catch them and sometimes we get swept away with them.

For example, you hear a noise outside so you start thinking about it or it could be that you just start thinking about what was on TV. You might be feeling anxious about something so up pops a thought. With thought can come powerful feelings and emotions. You start thinking about something that once happened to you and you start to feel happy, sad or angry.

Sometimes we need to understand and try to control our thoughts in order to gain peace. Imagine that someone you know plays a trick on you. You begin feeling angry which then provides for the blowing up of a thought balloon, which is about you getting your revenge. The bigger this thought becomes the more you start to generate negative emotions until the thought becomes so huge that, like the pack of balloons at the fairground, it starts to carry you away to a place that you might not want to be; to getting your revenge. So sometimes we need to be able to let go of thought. This is not easy and this is why we are going to practice it in our session here. If we can let negative thought go, we could place something much more wholesome such as calm in its place.

You might like to make use of the following questions in order to explore the issue further:

▸ Can we learn to control our thoughts, especially when they are very powerful?

▸ Do we have much control over powerful thoughts that threaten to overwhelm us?

▸ Do we always have to do what our thoughts tell us, particularly when they are angry ones?

Visualisation exercise

Initiate the relaxation exercise or your own suitable method.

Now you can begin and complete the visualisation exercise by reciting the following words to the children:

Now you are relaxed I want you to turn your attention to your thoughts for a moment. Without trying too hard see what kind of thoughts come into your mind whether they are generated by the things from the outside or inside world. Just watch them. See which are the thoughts that come and go quickly and which are the ones that stay.

(Pause)

Now that you have done that, I want you to try to let any thought that comes into your mind just pass again, in other words don't take hold of it. For instance, instead of going along with the thought, 'I am hungry,' just let it pass. Don't try too hard. Just let go of it. Whatever kind of thoughts comes into your mind just let go of them, whether they are good or bad. Try not to follow them through. If you do start thinking something through then see if you can let it go like you would a balloon. If lots of different thoughts come into your head then you can simply focus on breathing gently and calmly until the many thoughts die down.

I will count from one to ten. At the end of the count you can slowly open your eyes. Once your eyes are open I want you to just gently adjust to what is around you. Don't jump up suddenly or start talking. I also want you appreciate any differences in how your body is feeling from the way it felt before. (Begin the count down.)

At the end of the exercise discuss with the class:

▸ How did this make you feel?
▸ Was it easy?
▸ What part was difficult?
▸ Could you use this relaxation method by yourself?

Use the 'My Thoughts' activity sheet to represent the feelings that were experienced by class members.

My Thoughts

Use the space below in any way you want to represent your thoughts.

Roar Of The Crowd

Sometimes children (and adults) find it hard to accept others help, love or support and praise. This exercise is to help them be more accepting to the idea that not everybody is out to harm them and some people want to help them make progress. The exercise also focuses on confidence-building and taking on challenges.

These questions can be used to promote further discussion:

‣ What is inner confidence?

‣ How can we gain it?

‣ How do we know when people have it?

‣ Why is it important to have and accept people's support?

Visualisation exercise

Initiate the relaxation exercise or your own suitable method.

Now you can begin and complete the visualisation exercise by reciting the following words to the children:

Imagine that you are in a race; a long distance running race. You can't see anyone else in sight. You don't know if you are front middle or back. You give your best effort and although you feel tired at times you won't give up. With each footstep you put down you start to feel really good about yourself because regardless of whether you are winning the race or not you are bringing out the best in yourself which makes you feel great. As you run on you begin to hear a noise that is getting steadily louder. You realise that it is the crowd cheering. They are cheering for you and clapping. All the people who you like and who like you are there. This makes you feel really good inside. This good feeling makes you pick up your feet with more purpose.

(Pause)

Your feet begin to move even quicker. With each step you take you begin to grow in confidence until you feel that you can take on any challenge in the world. You are near the end: you see the tape and you burst through it. The crowd cheers more loudly than ever. You see a stand with a golden trophy encrusted with pearls. It is your deserved prize for your best effort. All the love and support from the crowd has gone into the cup and is making the pearls shine with the brightness of ten moons.

(Pause)

You go and pick it up. As soon as you pick it up it sends out a good feeling that starts going through your hands and then starts working its way through your entire body.

You are getting so much good energy from this cup that you can spare a little.

Send a little of this good energy in whatever form you can to a place, person or persons that you think might benefit from it.

(When you feel the children are ready begin the count out).

I will count from one to ten. At the end of the count you can slowly open your eyes. Once your eyes are open I want you to just gently adjust to what is around you. Don't jump up suddenly or start talking. I also want you appreciate any differences in how your body is feeling from the way it felt before. (Begin the count down.)

At the end of the exercise discuss with the class:

▸ How did this make you feel?

▸ Was it easy?

▸ Which part was difficult?

▸ Could you use this relaxation method by yourself?

Use the 'Good Energy' activity sheet to represent the feelings that were experienced by class members.

Good Energy

Use the space below in any way you want to
represent your good energy.

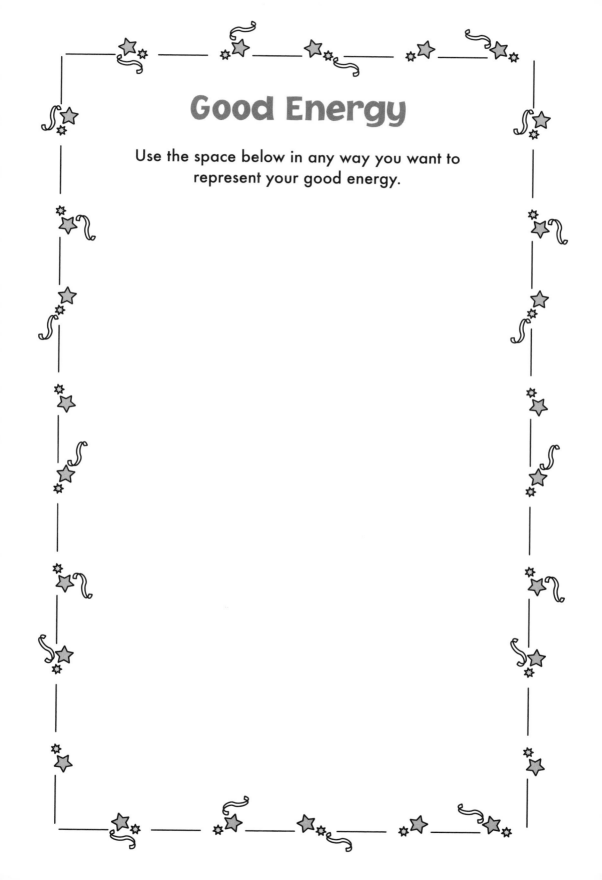

Quick Fixes and Tune-ups

For this section you don't have to initiate any deep relaxation
technique because of the nature of the exercises.

Bow And Arrow

This is a visualisation exercise for dispersing of negative feelings.

Use the activity sheet 'Negative Feelings' at the end of the session.

Deep relaxation technique is not recommended because this exercise concentrates on raising and bringing to the fore negative emotions.

The following questions touch on the issue of negativity:

▸ What do we mean by negative feelings?
▸ Is it a good thing to hold onto negative feelings?
▸ What is the effect, if any, of holding onto negative feeling?

As an exercise to be carried out beforehand the children can fill out the activity sheet 'Negative Feelings' which encourages them to write on the lines of an arrow the feelings they would like to disperse of whatever they may be.

It may be worthwhile exploring the issue as to whether some feelings, such as anger, are always 'bad'. For instance, it can be natural to feel angry if someone mistreats you. It is usually when feelings get out of control that they are deemed truly negative. You may also include as part of the discussion the idea that when we have a visual model of dispersing something like anger it can help us reach a goal of peace much more quickly.

Say to the children:

We are going to consider negative feelings. Let us go around the room and consider the different types of negative feelings that there can be. For example, wanting to physically hurt someone else because you have fallen out with them or thinking that you are not as 'good' as other people or that you are inferior because you don't always have the newest style of training shoes, clothing or latest model of a game.

Exercise

Think of some feeling that you would like to get rid of. For example, there are a lot of feelings that can make us feel bad and stop us becoming the person that we could be. There are feelings such as anger, fear, anxiety and shame, to name a few. I want you to imagine how this makes you feel. I want you to think about how it sometimes trips you up.

Now I want you to imagine that there is a bow and arrow in front of you. You take up the bow first and then you reach for the arrow. As soon as you touch the arrow you realise it is a magic one because it starts to draw all the negative emotion out of you and into itself. There is a target some distance ahead of you. It is a bale of hay. As you load the bow I want you to keep projecting into it all the negative emotion that you want to get rid of. When you have done as much of this as you can I want you to fire the arrow. Visualise the arrow going into the hay. On impact imagine all the negative energy from the arrow being absorbed by the hay.

I will count from one to ten. At the end of the count you can slowly open your eyes. Once your eyes are open I want you to just gently adjust to what is around you. Don't jump up suddenly or start talking. I also want you appreciate any differences in how your body is feeling from the way it felt before. (Begin the count down.)

At the end of the exercise discuss with the class:

‣ How did this make you feel?
‣ Was it easy?

▸   Which part was difficult?

▸   Could you use this relaxation method by yourself?

negative Feelings

Write any negative feelings or emotions that you would like to get rid of on the lines of the arrow.

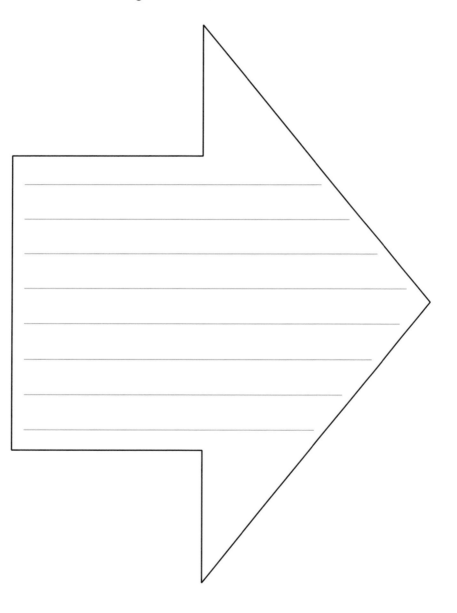

The Tap

The following exercise is concerned with turning off negative emotions. It also touches on recognising choice in going with or against an emotion.

This exercise is about encouraging children to appreciate that they can turn off negative feelings that threaten to overwhelm them. This provides them with a visual model in order to help structure self-control. Although the exercise has anger as its focus in this instance, it can be used as a model for controlling other emotions such as anxiety and fear, when the need arises.

▸ What happens when we have negative feelings?
▸ Can we turn off negative feelings before we allow them to turn into negative action?

Exercise

The aim of this particular exercise is to help you to try to deal with negative emotion. All types of emotion have their place. There are times when it is all right to be angry, sad or anxious although these are usually thought of as negative. However, what is not all right is when these emotions get the better of us and threaten to carry us away like a boat in the middle of rough water. That is when they become negative. Sometimes visual and symbolic models of the emotional state that we want to reach can be useful. By thinking peaceful thoughts this can bring us to a more peaceful state.

I want you to close your eyes. Imagine as clearly as you can a situation that made you feel angry or negative. Think of this anger as being a river of water where the water is rough. You can turn off this negative wave of energy. Imagine you see a tap from which the rough water is emerging. Follow the course of the water. You see the tap at the end of it. You start to turn the tap. The more you turn it the slower the water becomes and the calmer you become, the more peaceful you become. Your heart beat becomes more gentle as does your breathing. You turn it and turn it until the water is just a trickle and you feel very calm.

I will count from one to ten. At the end of the count you can slowly open your eyes. Once your eyes are open I want you to gently adjust to what is around you. Don't jump up suddenly or start talking. I also want you appreciate any differences in how your body is feeling from the way it felt before. (Begin the count down.)

At the end of the exercise discuss with the class:

- How did this make you feel?
- Was it easy?
- Which part was difficult?
- Could you use this relaxation method by yourself?

The class members can now do 'The Tap' activity sheet.

The Tap

Use the space below to can show all the negative
thoughts and feelings coming out of the tap.

Receptive Hands

This involves opening up to learning challenges.

Ask the questions:

▸ What does an open attitude towards learning mean?
▸ What happens when we have a closed mind?

I have employed this technique when children are negative about particular subjects. I employ it when I hear the cry 'I hate.' When this question of the hate is explored it often emerges that what the child is responding to is their lack of confidence rather than the subject. So I would ask them to do the following exercise but not from a point of view of forcing them to like what they say they hate - such a position will only make their feeling more entrenched and resistant - but from a spirit of open exploration out of which can come the possibility of discovering that they might like the subject, which is often what happens.

It is worthwhile explaining to them that immediate negative reactions without thought can create a type of brick wall in the mind that will automatically block discovery of possibilities. That is why people such as athletes don't take a negative stance because it is so easy for negative results to follow hard on the heels of negative thinking.

This exercise also gives them a conceptual framework for thinking about how their minds work psychologically.

The technique is simple and doesn't need to involve any deep relaxation.

Ask the children to close their eyes and imagine that their minds which collect all their knowledge are a pair of hands. Ask them to visualise the image as clearly as possible. Ask them to imagine those hands opening up. Tell them that this represents a positive statement to try to get the most out of the subject, and to tackle the subject in a spirit of generosity.

Along with this exercise ask them to substitute, 'I hate this,' with words such as, 'Although this may not be my favourite area I will try to be positive because I may find something about the subject that I enjoy.'

This technique also offers a model of how to treat the challenging aspects of life so that instead of something to run away from or fear they will gain confidence in knowing they can make gains from challenges.

I will count from one to ten. At the end of the count you can slowly open your eyes. Once your eyes are open I want you to just gently adjust to what is around you. Don't jump up suddenly or start talking. I also want you appreciate any differences in how your body is feeling from the way it felt before. (Begin the count down.)

At the end of the exercise discuss with the class:

- How did this make you feel?
- Was it easy?
- Which part was difficult?
- Could you use this relaxation method by yourself?

The class can now do the 'Receptive Hands' activity sheet.

Receptive Hands

In the hand shapes below show the areas of you that you could be more positive about.

Tests and Exams

Tests and exams are unavoidable and they have crept more and more into the primary sector. The following is an exercise that has been created in order to help children to relax when confronted by them.

A few days before the exam ask them to practice breathing slowly and fully (from the diaphragm). Good relaxation goes with a fuller breath. Shallow breathing increases nervousness. Tell the children that they are going to do a projection based on feeling relaxed before and during the exam.

Exercise

Close your eyes. I want you to use your imagination and imagine that when you wake up on the day of the exam, instead of dreading the day, you are going to wake up and look forward to the challenge.

Imagine that there is a big smile on your face, that you are breathing deeply and you feel good because you will try your best and your best is all you can do. Visualise yourself with a light step as you go abut your preparations for getting ready to go to school. Imagine yourself feeling warm from the inside as you do on a warm and sunny day. Now imagine yourself at the exam table feeling really relaxed. Checking your breathing, you realise you are breathing calmly. Create a clear image of yourself writing with confidence, doing your best and feeling good about yourself doing your best.

I will count from one to ten. At the end of the count you can slowly open your eyes. Once your eyes are open I want you to gently adjust to what is around you. Don't jump up suddenly or start talking. I also want you appreciate any differences in how your body is feeling from the way it felt before. (Begin the count down.)

At the end of the exercise discuss with the class:

▸ How did this make you feel?
▸ Was it easy?
▸ Which part was difficult?
▸ Could you use this relaxation method by yourself?

Start of Day Positive Focus

The following two exercises are concerned with helping the group or class to start the day or part of the day on a positive note. They are intended to be very quick.

Here are a few questions that you can ask in order to start the ball rolling:

▸ How does helping others to feel good about themselves help the world?

▸ When we help others to feel good do we derive any benefits ourselves?

Positive Focus One

Discuss with the children how it is easier to maintain peace and goodwill towards oneself and others if they already have a vision of it or have it as a goal, instead of taking it for granted. Inform them that this is called being proactive.

Tell the children that they are going to work towards projecting a positive image of themselves onto the day.

The activity sheet 'My Positive Picture' can be used before or after the imagining.

Now you can begin and complete the visualisation exercise by reciting the following words to the children:

Close your eyes. You are an artist. I want you to imagine roughly the day ahead. The day ahead is going to be like your canvas. I want you to draw or paint a picture in your mind of a positive image of yourself and all the things you want for the day.

Think about:

- how you want to feel during the day
- how you would like to treat others
- how you want to carry yourself
- how you want to be treated.

Positive Focus Two

This exercise is based on generating goodwill towards the individual as well as the group at the start of the day or a part of the day. It concentrates on bringing positive aspects of the children's lives to the fore. This will help them to keep in the forefront of their mind their own sense of 'goodness.' It will also give them a goal of remaining positive.

Say to the children:

Close your eyes. Imagine there is a spark in your heart. Colour this spark of light your favourite colour. This spark of light is going to grow. To make it grow you have to think of all the good things you associate with yourself and with your life. You can summon up any memory of something nice, good or positive that happened to you.

Now every positive thought you summon up is going to make the spark grow and grow until the glow is as big as you are. It is like putting money in a piggy bank until you fill it. However in this case you are filling yourself with positive things. Once this glow is as large as your whole body I want you to have an imaginary forecast of the day in as much detail as possible. Imagine that you have this glow throughout the day keeping you warm, secure and self-assured.

I will count from one to ten. At the end of the count you can slowly open your eyes. Once your eyes are open I want you to gently adjust to what is around you. Don't jump up suddenly or start talking. I also want you appreciate any differences in how your body is feeling from the way it felt before. (Begin the count).

At the end of the exercise discuss with the class:

▶ How did this make you feel?
▶ Was it easy?
▶ Which part was difficult?
▶ Could you use this relaxation method by yourself?

My Positive Picture

Imagine that you are an artist who can make anything that you paint or write about real. The day, as it is about to unfold, is your canvas.

Draw and write about a positive picture of yourself as you would like to be seen throughout the day.

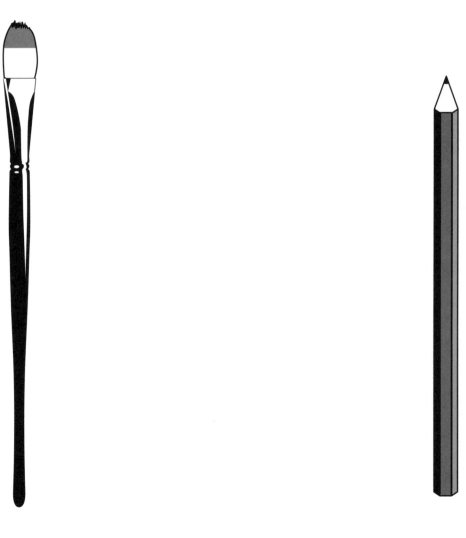

Ball Of Light

This exercise is useful for children who have difficulty gelling with one another and who are constantly bickering. It is also ideal for the promotion of goodwill that exists amongst a class.

The following question and statement can help to introduce the task:

▸ What does good will toward others mean?
▸ When there is general goodwill all can benefit.

Use the activity sheet 'The Ball of Light' before or after the activity.

You will need one soft ball - a juggling ball, sponge ball or tennis ball will do.

Tell the children that they are going to play a ball game. This game will help them to try to be positive with one another. It is like a handshake but instead they are going to use a ball. They are going to help to make each other feel really good about themselves. Perhaps one of the best things that anybody can do in this world is to try to make another person feel good about themselves. So you are going to carry out this very important task.

Ask the children to get into a circle and then sit down. Explain to the children that before they can play this game they need to transform the ball from an ordinary ball to one that is magical and special. Explain that the special ball will help everyone to feel good about themselves and each other.

Introduce the ball into the middle of the circle. Explain to the children that in order to turn this ordinary ball into a special one they need to think of all the positive thoughts and feelings they can and then imagine them going into the ball. Give them examples. For instance:

▶ 'Remember the feeling you had when someone gave you a big hug or a lovely present.'

▶ 'Remember when someone said something really nice to you.'

▶ 'Can you recall a time when you felt really special?'

Explain to the children that everyone is going to sit quietly and focus all this positive energy and feeling onto this ball for a few minutes in silence.

Spend about two minutes on this or as much time as you think they will need, without them breaking the atmosphere of calm focus. Try not to allow the children to become restless.

After this period is over, tell the children that the ball has now been positively charged (just like a battery) with their warm feelings so that it can carry their goodwill to each and everyone in the class.

Ask the children to stand up and maintain the circle. In turn, each person is going to look for children who are giving them friendly eye contact and without rushing will throw the ball to them. The ball must be thrown under arm in a gentle manner. The child then throws the ball saying the name of the person to whom the ball is being thrown. When the child throws the ball she must freeze in the posture they find themselves holding after the release of the ball. The thrower can only relax when the recipient of the ball says thank you. And so the game goes on. Make sure everyone gets a turn to be recipient and thrower.

Ensure that the game is played calmly. Children are not allowed to call for the ball, a situation that can build up angry feelings when a child who is calling for the ball isn't chosen.

At the end of the exercise discuss with the class:

▸   How did this make you feel?
▸   Was it easy?
▸   Which part was difficult?

The Ball of Light

We all like to feel appreciated and valued. Write on the ball of light things you could do to brighten up another person's day.

From Buds To Flowers

This session focuses on working towards a wholesome vision of who we would like to be.

You might like to explore the following questions with the children:

▸ What type of person would you like to become in the future?
▸ What elements (internal and external) do you need in order to help you become this person?

The following is a statement that you can use to reinforce the discussion.

A bud contains the potential to be a flower. A caterpillar contains the potential to be a butterfly. As human beings we are quite lucky in that we have the potential to be a great many things. The sooner that we can develop a vision of who or what we would like to be the more readily we can work towards this, particularly whilst we are still in the cocoon stage. Thinking about our future self involves thinking about the type of people that we would like to be.

In order for the potential flower to be at its best when developing from a seed it has certain requirements such as the need for good soil, water and sunlight. What it becomes is a result of what goes into it.

We need to attend to ourselves and feed ourselves with the vision of who we would like to be as well as have a generous attitude towards ourselves.

In thinking about your future self you can start to develop your own visualisations on the type of person that you would like to be. What you put into yourself now you can reap the benefits of later.

After completion of the 'From a Bud to a Flower' activity sheet, discuss with the class:

▸   What major change do they think will happen in the world in the next ten years?

▸   What do they think they will be doing in ten years?

▸   What are they going to try to develop in themselves in the next ten years?

From a Bud a Flower

Think of the type of person you would like to work towards becoming.

Write down your ideas on the various parts of the flower.

Bibliography

Ballard, J. (1982) *Circlebook*, Irvington, New York.

Bliss, T., Robinson, G., & Maines, B. (1995) *Developing Circle Time*, Lucky Duck Publishing Ltd, Bristol.

Bliss, T. & Tetley, J. (1993) *Circle Time*, Lucky Duck Publishing Ltd, Bristol.

Gawain & Shakti. (2004) *Creative Visualisation*, 25th Anniversary edition, Nataraj Publishing, USA.

Lang, P. (1998) *Getting Round to Clarity: What do we mean by Circle Time?* Pastoral Care in Education 16, 3, 3-10.

Markham, U. (1981) Hypnothink: *The revolutionary way to reprogramme your mind for success,* 3rd impression , Thorsons Publishing Group, UK.

National Healthy School Status - A Guide for School (2005) Department of Health.

Syer, J. & Connolly, C. (1998) *Sporting Body Sporting Mind: an athlete's guide to mental training,* 3rd edition, Simon and Schuster, London.

Taylor, M. S. (2003) *Going Round In Circles*, NFER.